First Edition

2018

Dedicated to the plant beings that whisper songs of healing and magick in my heart.

TABLE OF CONTENTS

BATH SALTS + SOAKS

Healing - Clearing - Cleansing.
Let the waters heal and cleanse you and purify
you. Let it wash away all your worries.. all your
doubts.. all your fears. Tell the waters what you
are afraid of and let her release it for you. Tell the
waters what you're most in love with, let her add
more to that love.
Rest in the sound. Rest in the bliss. Rest in the
healing waters of love.

We all must continue to release + let go of things
that no longer serves our TRUEST + Highest
SELVES. The Full Moon is a perfect time to release
all that is holding you back from your potential-
self and for celebrating the path traveled and
danced upon. The New moon is a perfect time to sit
with yourself and plant seeds of intention. It's all
about new beginnings, cleansing your soul, altar,
life, or whatever may be holding grudges or
negative energy. Gather your thoughts and plan
for this cycle.

As you are soaking, you can sing/chant this
mantra - - - "I RELEASE CONTROL AND
SURRENDER TO THE FLOW OF LOVE THAT WILL
HEAL ME" --- keep repeating until you feel the
magick working within you, and around you.

MNI WICONI
WATER IS LIFE

PERSEPHONE CITRUS BATH SOAK

epsom salts . lavender . rose petals . orange citrus peels. white sage leaves . quartz crystals

GODDESS OF MIDSUMMER BATH SOAK

epsom salts . sea salts . himalayan salt . whole dried calendula flowers . dried lavender flowers . lavender essential oils . ylang ylang essential oils

HATHOR
BATH SOAK

epsom salt . himalayan pink
salt . red rose petals .
frankincense oil . rose
absolute . lavender oil .

MILK GODDESS
BATH SOAK

dehydrated coconut milk .
organic baking soda .
chamomile flowers . vanilla
essential oil .

VILA GODDESS
BATH SOAK

epsom salt . pink himalayan
sea salt . organic white sage
leaves + sage essential oil .
organic hibiscus leaves . ceda
essential oil

GODDESS OF SILENCE BATH SOAK

ench grey sea salt . sea clay
essential oils of: eucalyptus
+ spearmint . himalayan sea
salt . salt of the dead sea .
coconut milk powder . wild-
harvested calendula flower
etals . rose petals . hibiscus
.

(optional)
ssentials oils of: sandalwood
. sweet orange . neroli

HERBAL FACIAL MASKS

Flowing - Fluttering - Flowering

We must all continue to practice sElf - love. The Goddess Grace whispers to me that there is a difference between having sElf - confidence and feeling secure. Ask yoursElf, "What makes ME feel secure?"
Imagine yourself as a flower. Let that visualization dance in your heart, feel the flowering and blossoming as you wake up each day and as you meet people throughout the day. Let each person see you as you truly are and experience your petals opening up to the sun that feeds you life.

Daily gentle exfoliation helps to gently remove the layer of dead skin cells, helping to clear your pores without destroying the balance of your skin's oils. Daily gentle exfoliation helps to reduce and minimize wrinkles and fine lines, while the soap-free skin-nourishing herbal ingredients provide your face with a healthy dose of the vitamins and minerals it's craving.

As you are exfolitating the dead skin away, you can sing/chant this mantra --- "I AM OPENING UP LIKE A LOTUS FLOWER - LET MY LOVE LIGHT SHINE IN THE DARKEST HOUR" --- keep repeating until you feel the magick working within you, and around you.

I AM A DELICATE FLOWER

CLEANSING GRAINS

calendula . oats . lavender .
roses . chamomile . coconut
sugar . coconut flour .
bentonite clay . rhassoul cla.
. rose hips . essential oil blen
of lavender + clove bud

I AM AN OPENING FLOWER CLEANSING GRAINS

rhassoul clay . rose petals . essential oils of lavender emongrass . carrot seed. gera um and helichrysum italicum

I AM A
HEALING FLOWER
CLEANSING GRAINS

french yellow clay . witch
hazel bark . essential oils of
lavender, carrot seed . tea
tree . lemon . german
chamomile

I AM
A FLUTTERING FLOWER
CLEANSING GRAINS

kaolin clay . bentonite clay
ground oats . ground almond .
poppy seeds . comfrey leaf .
lavender buds . rose petals .
calendula flowers . essential
oils of lavender + rose

I AM
A FLOWING FLOWER
CLEANSING GRAINS

bentonite clay . actived
charcoal . dried chamomile
flower . dried lavender buds
. dried rose petals . dried
calendula flowers
. essential oils of lavender
+ rose + grapeseed .

LIP + BODY SCRUBS

Blossoming - Blooming - Beautiful

Know that everything you do can be witchcraft. Creatin
Self-care and Self-love rituals for yourself is considered
witchcraft. Know that you have the tools within you to
create peace within and that you never have to look outsi
of yourself for peace... or love or healing or anything tha
you feel is lacking within. Everything that you seek, yo
have within you. You are A POWERFUL BADASS WITCI
Wave your wand, cast your spells, put your heart and spi
into your ritual, and believe in the magick that you are
creating.

As you are exfolitating the dead skin away, you can
sing/chant this mantra --- "EARTH MY BODY, WATER M
BLOOD, AIR MY BREATH & FIRE MY SPIRIT" --- keep
repeating until you feel the magick working within you, a
around you.

GLAMOUR SPELLS
LIP SCRUB

eeswax . coconut oil . sweet
almond oil . shea butter,
itamin E and pure essential
oils.

- optional flavors -

rosemary + vanilla
mint + sage
coconut + rose
lavender + honey

GLOW SPELLS
BODY SCRUB

organic cane sugar . raw
organic honey . coconut oil .
sweet almond oil . shea butte
. vitamin E oil . orange oil .
lemon oil.

AYURVEDIC SPELLS
BODY SCRUB

sea salt . jojoba oil . coconut
oil . shea butter . vitamin E .
curmeric root powder . neem
oil . pink grapefruit essential
oil . rosemary

GODDESS SPELLS
BODY SCRUB

vanilla extract . coconut oil
shea butter . sweet almond oi
. avocado oil . vitamin E oil .
cane sugar . walnut shells .
himalayan sea salt .

SISTERS OF THE ROSE LINEAGE BODY SCRUB

sea salt . organic sucrose . coconut oil . shea butter . weet almond oil . avocado oil caprylic/capric triglycerides rose clay . buckthorn extract aloe vera extract . rosemary

ANTIOXIDANT COFFEE BODY SCRUB

coffee . cinnamon . brown
sugar . coconut oil. jojoba oil
extra virgin olive oil . water
vanilla extract

GAIA SPELLS
BODY SCRUB

rganic cane sugar . dead sea
alt . virgin coconut oil . fair
trade coffee . shea butter .
ango butter . pure vitamin E
. poppy seeds . rosehip
essential oils

HERBAL TEAS

History of Tea and Magick Lore

...ul Coelho, author of The Alchemist, wrote ...ea Ceremony is a way of worshipping the ...autiful and the simple. All one's efforts are concentrated on trying to achieve ...fection through the imperfect gestures of daily life. It's beauty consists in the ...spect with which it performed. If a mere ...up of tea can bring us closer to God, we ...hould watch out for all the other dozen opportunities that each ordinary day offers."

...ea Magick is ANCIENT and is also a very ...owerful form of Witchcraft. Tea Witches ...e considered ZEN AF yet very powerful at ... same time. They are not only herbalists, ...ut through the magick of the herbs they ...ve found a way to ground themselves and ...hieve wisdom. It's no wonder that monks ...nd wise hermits choose tea over coffee. ...ffee is a very magickal as well). Yet, The ...erbs have a different language that they ...eak, and when we begin to really listen to their songs and whispers, we begin to ...reflect and mirror the magick they hold within.

...ITCH TIP: use the dried herbs in the tea bags for divination or for other herbal ...gick. This is a great way to save money if you usually purchase herbs.

DIVINE FEMININE BALANCING

raspberry leaf . yarrow . oat straw . nettle . orange peel . fennel . alfalfa . red clover . rose petal . lemon balm . hibiscus . spearmint

DIVINE FEMININE RISING

tulsi, peppermint, calendula, orange peel, dandelion root

DIVINE FEMININE FLOURISHING

lemon verbena,
chamomile, passion
flower, calendula, rose

DIVINE FEMININE NOURISHING

raspberry leaf, nettle,
rose hips, chamomile, red
clover, shatavri

DIVINE FEMININE FERTILITY

raspberry leaf, nettle, red clover lemon balm . oat straw . alfalfa . skullcap . love

DIVINE FEMININE MOON CYCLE

motherwort leaf . red raspberry leaf . chickweed . skullcap . rose . sage leaf . white-leaved savory . passionflower leaf . calendula .

SLEEPING GODDESS TEA

hops . valerian . passionflower . spearmint .

GLOWING GODDESS TEA

rooibos . cinnamon bark . cocoa shell . cardamom seeds . vanilla bean . nettle leaf . licorice root . mullein leaf . schisandra berry .

LUNAR GODDESS TEA

passionflower . dong quai . damiana . resehips . schisandra

HERBAL PILLOWS

)))) 🌑 ⬤ ⬤ ⬤

Herb Pillows for Spell-work

potent time to make a sachet is during the Dark
on - make small bags filled with elements of the
rth and wear on you until they fall off, no longer
ed the sachet, or until the next Dark moon, but
emember to keep it hidden from muggles. Herb
hets can be hung above your bed or placed inside
your pillow sheet.

witch tip
use coffee filters for sachets

; two pieces of material in a color that is specific
our dream, desire or spell. Sew three of the sides
ng a color that corresponds with your spell, while
iving one edge unsewn to add your contents into
the bag.
ditional items: roots, dirt, herbs, coins, crystals.
(anything that supports your main intention.

imple for an Abundance bag: 3 coins and 3 pieces
ginger with a handmade sigil for abundance, also
d something that represents yourself, like a few
ands of your hair or writing your name on a piece
f paper and folding it three times. Breathe your
eath into the bag after adding your contents and
en sew it up or tie with a ribbon. Tap it 3 times to
tivate its magick. Feed the bag with an essential
. like rosemary or anything you feel corresponds
h the dark moon, new beginnings, and activation.

HERBS

Lavender:
sleep, peace, dreams, relaxation, protection, happiness, healing,
anti-stress & anxiety
Rosemary:
sleep, peace, dreams, protection, healing, anti- stress, wards off bad
dreams & negativity
Sea salt:
protection, banishing, cleansing, purifying
Hops flowers: sleep, healing, anti-anxiety, stops restlessness
Sugar:
for extra sweetness
Jasmine:
calming, relaxation, prophetic dreams, love
Chamomile:
sleep, peace, protection, healing, relaxation, anti-stress & anxiety,
wards off bad dreams & nightmares
Mugwort:
dreams, protection, healing, astral projection
Thyme:
sleep, dreams, healing, protection, wards off bad dreams
Peppermint:
sleep, dreams, healing, protection, happiness, anti-stress & anxiety,
purification
Valerian:
calming, protection, deep restful sleep
Vervain:
peace, protection, wards off bad dreams & nightmares
Hyssop:
purification and protection.
Cedar:
healing, purification, money and protection.
Basil:
love, exorcism, wealth, protection and courage.
Dandelion:
Divination, Wishes and Calling Spirits.

CRYSTALS

Amethyst
peace, calming, relieves insomnia, wards off bad dreams &
nightmares, prevents oversleeping, stabilizes physical, mental &
emotional being. Activates crown chakra.

Blue lace agate
peace, calming, healing, calms the mind, reduces stress &
anxiety.

Smoky Quartz
protection, calming, relieves insomnia, wards off bad dreams,
nightmares & negativity.

Fluorite
peace, protection, protects against stress & negativity,
stabilizes emotions, calms the mind.

Rose Quartz
calming, peace, healing, calms emotions & rids of negativity,
deep & restful sleep, relieves insomnia, relaxation, brings sweet
dreams + activates the heart chakra.

Black Tourmaline
protection against negative energy, curses, malicious entities &
general feelings of being overwhelmed.

Black Obsidian
ultimate prevailer of truth, to find & protect your own inner
truth. Cleanses negative energy.

Selenite
selenite is self cleansing & also may be used to cleanse other
crystals. Angelic magic, wisdom, emotions + creativity.

PROTECTION

hyssop . lavender . sage .
obsidian . tourmaline . basil
. cedar . sea salt

UNCONDITIONAL LOVE

lavender . selenite . rose
quartz . myrrh . sage . sugar

POSITIVITY

rosemary . sunflower . basil
. blue lace agate . clear
quartz .

RELAXATION AID

lavender . rosemary . thyme .
rose petal . yarrow .
rose quartz

SLEEP AID

lavender . mugwort .
peppermint . mint .
chamomile . selenite . smoky
quartz

ANXIETY AID

passionflower . lavender .
ashwaganda . lemon balm .
blue lace agate . tourmaline .

HERBAL CEREMONY BLEND

))))◗●●●●

e smoking of all herbs should be done in respect and in ceremony.

Dose with proper concern.
is very important that you do the proper research to ee if you can smoke a certain herb. Also if you start feeling sick after smoking it cease use of it mediately. You may be fine ingesting a certain herb, ut you could have an allergy to smoking said herb. lease note that some of these could be poisonous if aten, we are speaking of smoking only. I also don't recommend replacing smoking herbs with getting medical treatment if you need assistance. Be very careful if you have health conditions.

Blends may be contraindicated during pregnancy.

For direct treatment of coughs and bronchial congestion, some herbs are smoked. This will provide immediate, but temporary relief for the condition. Unlike Tobacco, the herbs which are smoked for therapeutic purposes contain no nicotine or other addicting substances. A small amount can be rolled as a joint, smoked in a pipe or water pipe. Lungs are filled with smoke, and fully exhaled. Inhale the smoke about 7 to 13 times for a single treatment.

commonly used herbs: coltsfoot, rosemary, mullein, yerba mate and sarsaparilla herb.

To aid in quitting smoking Tobacco; Lobelia, Indian Tobacco is smoked. It contains Lobeline. Lobeline is an alkaloid found in a variety of plants, particularly those in the family of Lobelia, including Indian tobacco, Devil's Tobacco, Cardinal flower, Great lobelia, Lobelia chinensis, and Hippobroma longiflora. Lobeline is very similar to nicotine but does not have the same set of effects, thus it reduces the sensation of need for nicotine, but does not provide the effects that lead to addictive smoking. Jimsonweed has been used extensively to treat asthma - this plant is extremely toxic in large doses and can cause severe near damage. Mugwort and catnip have been smoked for their calming aids to treat sleep deprivation and restlessness. Damiana has been used for its aphrodisiac effects. Peppermint is added to smoking blends for its cooling properties and Licorice is added for its sweet flavor.

SPINNING COYOTE CEREMONY BLEND

NSOMNIA - REDUCE GANJA SMOKE - ANXIETY AID

mullein - one half cup
skullcap - one quarter
passionflower - one quarter
manzanita - one eighth cup
damiana - one eighth cup
fennel seed - sprinkle

TAKE IT EASY
CEREMONY BLEND

IF YOU'RE FEELING DEPRESSED, SMOKE
SPINNING COYOTE INSTEAD

hops - one half cup
mullein - one quarter cup
skullcap - one eighth cup
manzanita - one eighth cup
deer's tongue - to taste
anise seed - sprinkle

CHAKRA ALIGNMENT CEREMONY BLEND

PSYCHIC ABILITES - INTRUSIVE
THOUGHT - MINDFULNESS

mullein - one half cup
skullcap - one quarter cup
damiana - one eighth cup
lavender - to taste
catnip - sprinkle

HYGIEIA HEALING CEREMONY BLEND

MENTAL CLARITY - CONCENTRATION

ginkgo - one half cup
mullein - one quarter cup
california poppy - one quarte
spearmint - one eighth cup
yerba mate - one eighth cup
lavender - to taste

HEKATE FIRE CEREMONY BLEND

LUNG HEALTH - NERVOUS SYSTEM

mullein - one half cup
skullcap - one quarter cup
uva ursi - one quarter
marshmallow - one eighth cup
damiana - one eighth cup
lobeila - sprinkle

SHAMANIC ASTRAL TRAVEL CEREMONY BLEND

LITERALLY FLY OFF TO ANOTHER DIMENSION.

mullein - one half cup
damiana - one quarter cup
mugwort - one quarter
chamomile - one eighth cup
valerian - one eighth cup
passionflower - one eighth cu
peppermint - sprinkle

SLEEPY CAT CEREMONY BLEND

MEOW LIKE A LAZY CAT . PASS OUT .
REST WELL .

hops - one half cup
catnip - one quarter cup
lemon balm - one quarter
chamomile - one eighth cup
valerian - one eighth cup

FULL MOON CEREMONY BLEND

CHANNEL THOSE FULL MOON VIBES .
RELEASE . GET WILD . OPEN YOUR HEA
TO THE ILLUMINATION OF THE MOON

mullein - one half cup
red raspberry - one quarter
cup
lemon balm - one quarter
rose petal - one eighth cup
chamomile - one eighth cup
salvia apiana- one eighth cup
lavender - sprinkle

NEW MOON CEREMONY BLEND

CHANNEL THOSE NEW MOON VIBES . GO
WITHIN . EMBODY THE SAGE ARCHETYPE
OPEN YOUR LOTUS FLOWER HEART TO
THE DARKNESS OF THE MOON .

mullein - one half cup
skullcap - one quarter cup
uva ursi - one quarter
marshmallow - one eighth cup
damiana - one eighth cup
lobeila - sprinkle

ECLIPSE PORTAL CEREMONY BLEND

TO HELP YOU STAY ROOTED LIKE A TREE DURING THE ECLIPSE PORTAL.

coltsfoot - one half cup
raspberry leaf - one quarter cup
mugwort - one quarter
yerba mate - one eighth cup
lavender - one eighth cup
rose petal - one eighth cup
white sage - one eighth cup

ROSEMARY MILK WITCH CEREMONY BLEND

ROSEMARY MILK WITCH'S FAVORITE
BLEND
APHRODIASIAC - VENUS - OSHUN VIBES

catnip - one half cup
skullcap - one quarter cup
rosemary - one quarter
rose petal - one eighth cup
damiana - one eighth cup
chamomile - one eighth cup
white sage - one eighth cup
lavender - sprinkle

YONI STEAM
BLENDS

Why We Steam

Yoni is a Sanskrit word meaning "vagina," "womb," "goddess" or "origin of life," and refers to the ENTIRE female reproductive system. Yoni steaming is intended to support all of these aspects of a woman.

Yoni steaming is a powerful ancient remedy that has been used for centuries by women worldwide to bring deep wellness, to help discover the root of the challenge, and promotes fast recovery. It is a holistic health practice in which a woman allows the warmth of herbal steam to gently permeate the exterior of her vagina. Heat improves circulation. When circulation is low, it creates stagnation, and stagnation is what results in cramps and pain. Many women experience reproductive health challenges in one form or another, from mild to severe menstrual cramps and irregular periods, to pain during intercourse, to challenges with conceiving a child. Often, women accept these challenges as normal, and rarely talk about the discomfort and suffering they feel because of the taboo that modern society has placed on this natural experience.

This wonderful and effective treatment i growing upon numbers of women who are seeking to naturally treat the root cause of these challenges, and heal their sacred womb temple. After just a few steams, women often report noticing reduced cramps, regulation of cycles, easier conception, and healing of abnormal tissues in and around the uterus. The Yoni is already self-cleansing and healing, however we still use Yoni steaming to add even more support to your yoni's magickal abilities The steam cleans everything. The steam cleans the yoni, the cervix, the uterus, the fallopian tubes, and the ovaries without even touching them.

YONI STEAMING:

Heals the womb
Improves The Menstrual Cycle
Deeply Connects Woman With Her Power
Source
Helps To Create Juicer Sex
Increases Fertility
Creates Sacred Ceremonial Space
Detoxifies

Vaginal Steam Benefits May ALSO Include:

Elimination of cramps
Clearing of bacteria or yeast infections
Draining painful cysts
Expelling fibroids
Resolving infertility
Postpartum Recovery (i.e. getting the body back to pre-pregnancy state, weight loss, lochia elimination, correcting prolapse/hemorrhoids, etc)
Miscarriage Recovery
Reduces Heavy Menstruation
Increases Scanty Menstruation
Returns Missing Periods
Regularizes long or short cycles to 28-30 days
Improves Vaginal Prolapse and Tightens Canal
Moisturizes Vaginal Dryness
Alleviates Painful Sex
Enhances Libido
Resolves PCOS
Treats Endometriosis
Odor elimination
Clearing up viruses and STDs
General Hygiene and Well-Being

CLEANSING HERBS

rose petals . white sage . lavender . parsley . witch hazel . chamomile . dandelion . mugwort . peppermint .

Designed for women on their cycle and who are postpartum - includes herbs to help clean out the uterus and improve blood circulation to the mid section. Balances the vaginal flora, improves the scent, tightens the skin, and nourishes the reproductive system. NOT FOR WOMEN WITH SHORT CYCLE (27 days or shorter) WOMEN WITH INTERIM BLEEDING - FRESH SPOTTING - SPONTANEOUS HEAVY BLEEDING BETWEEN CYCLES. Suitable for: postpartum users - users with missing period - recovering from miscarriage - normal or long menstrual cycles (Cycle = 28 days or longer Missing Cycle) - Oral Contraceptive users

GENTLE HERBS

chamomile . citrus peel .
astragalus . cornsilk .
peppermint . parsley .
mugwort

Designed for women with short cycles who have
interim bleeding... continual fresh spotting...
heavy bleeding between periods. IF YOU FALL
INTO ANY OF THESE CATEGORIES THESE ARE
THE MOST IMPORTANT HERBS TO STEAM WITH.
Suitable for: users prone to short cycles (Cycle =
27 days or less) - interim bleeding (fresh spotting
between periods/ spontaneous bleeding) anytime
in the past 3 months - experiencing two periods
per month, anytime in the past 3 months -
Underage 13

DISINFECTING HERBS

white sage . sophora root. cornsilk . parsley .

Designed for women that have experienced active infections or viruses over the past 3 months. Includes herbs that help fight bacteria, Yeast Infections, Bacterial Infections, and Viruses while expelling toxins, reducing inflammation, getting rid of excess mucus, deodorizing and resetting the healthy vaginal flora in the reproductive tract. IF YOU HAVE ANY OF THE ABOVE ALONG WITH A SHORT MENSES (27 days or less) THEN GET BOTH DISINFECTING HERBS + GENTLE HERBS

COOLING HERBS

irish moss . white peony root . and other herbs

Designed for women experiencing: Vaginal Dryness, living in Hot Climates, Night Sweats/Hot Flashes. Included are herbs that help to nourish, moisturize, and cool down, as well as tonify the kidneys and provide circulation.

LEARN MORE ABOUT YONI STEAMING WITH JEDAYA BARBOZA

priestessjedaya.weebly.com

SERUMS + SALVES

SERUMS

HOW TO USE:

Apply 7-13 drops to cleansed skin i
the early rising and night. Massag
into skin, and allow 1-3 minutes to
absorb before applying makeup.

For a hydrating night treatment:
Apply a generous amount of drops t
skin before bed, we recommend
being pretty generous and using 13
22 drops. Massage into skin, and ge
some beauty rest. Awaken to result
you'll adore.

Apricot Kernel Oil is quickly absorbed, and is especially known for its ability to repair damaged skin cells. It aids in decreasing eye puffiness, and nourishes dry, parched skin, leaving it soft and supple.

Virgin Chia Seed Oil is derived from the ancient superfood Chia, which is the richest botanical source of Omega 3 fatty acids found in nature. Chia is a powerful source of Alpha Lipoic Acid, a powerful antioxidant that helps minimize fine lines, wrinkles, and enlarged pores. It also has a reputation for increasing skins hydration significantly.

Calendula is a delicate, yet effective botanical. Calendula stimulates the production of collagen around wound sites, and works to soothe and minimize scarring. It is especially effective on thread veins, tiny broken veins on the skin.

Hibiscus has a magical reputation because of its natural ability to tone and firm skin. It is known to speed up cell-turnover, encouraging smoother, more youthful skin.

Moroccan Rose is a rare and stunning rose that has a high amount of antioxidant properties. It is known for being the "Queen of essential oils", and for good reason. Rose oil has high levels of antioxidant properties that can fight signs of aging and gives dry skin a surge of moisture.

Jasmine Oil is derived from the Night Blooming Jasmine flower and has a strong, yet sweet, exquisite aroma. Jasmine is known for its calming effect on skin, and is especially beneficial on dehydrated skin. It also contains high amounts of skin softening properties, leaving skin next level smooth.

Silk powder is produced from high quality silk of the cocoon of the silk worm, silk powder retains the chemical properties of the raw material. This extraction is 100% fibroin, which contains 18 different amino acids and trace elements essential to the human body. An ideal protein enricher, silk powder helps maintain moisture levels in the skin and hair and prevents dryness. Its crystalline structure reflects light. In skin care products, this quality improves luminescence and elasticity. Silk powder possesses a chemical composition that is very close to that of human skin and hair, making it a wonderful source of nourishment and maintenance. Its natural glossy property will give your face a smooth feel and appearance.

Perilla seed oil is rich in vitamins and amino acids. Approximately 50-60% of perilla seed oil is alpha-linolenic acid (ALA), an omega-3 fatty acid. This high ALA content helps skin retain moisture. The omega-3 fatty acids are polyunsaturated fatty acids known to revitalize and improve the appearance and texture of skin.

Oat oil is soothing and highly emollient, oat oil absorbs slowly, but has a very rich feel like liquid silk. This oil is wonderfully rich in antioxidants and tocopherols with natural emulsifiers.

Marula oil is a botanical treasure indigenous to the Miombo woodlands of Southern and West Africa, the Marula tree is a medium-sized dioecious tree. The raw materials for the oil have been harvested and pressed by community collectives of mostly women. Marula oil, rich in antioxidant and essential fatty acids (good, healthy fats), has been found to significantly improve the hydration, softness and smoothness of skin. Absorbs easily, leaving a silky smooth feel.

Sacha inchi oil is obtained from the organic seeds of the sacha inchi plant, indigenous to the Peruvian Amazon Rainforest. The cold pressed oil is one of the richest vegetable sources of polyunsaturated fatty acids, namely alpha-linolenic acid (omega 3), linolenic acid (omega 6), and oleic acid (omega 9). Boasts exceptionally high antioxidant properties. Sacha inchi will soothe dry, damaged skin and reduce the appearance of fine lines and wrinkles. Lightweight and absorbs quickly without leaving an oily residue.

Patchouli is an amazing essential oil tonic for skin.

Sage imparts a fresh feel.

Rice bran oil is extracted from the bran or outer coat of the brown rice grain removed during the milling process. Rich in vitamins, minerals, proteins and essential oils, rice bran oil also contains a constituent called gamma-oryzanol, which is known to be safe to use in formulations meant for outdoor use. Contains a high percentage of fatty acids and unsaponifiables and is one of the best sources of tocotrienols, an antioxidant that may be much more powerful and effective than vitamin E. Gamma-oryzanol, which is used in many types of sunscreen products, adds sheen while moisturizing and conditioning the skin without weighing it down.

Hemp seed oil repairs dry skin, providing hydration. With a high concentration of omega 3 and omega 6 essential fatty acids, hemp seed oil has a full amino acid spectrum. This means that it provides complete protein and possesses a high mineral content. Due to its high content of proteins and essential fatty acids, hemp seed oil can be used to nourish the skin and hair.

Flax seed oil is an extremely rich emollient high in essential fatty acids, alpha-linolenic acids, vitamins E and B, and minerals, flax seed oil nourishes skin leaving it dewy and hydrated.

Rosemary antioxidant encourages cellular metabolism of skin and protects against free radicals.

Ylang ylang is a wonderful essential oil for mature skin.

Carrot seed detoxifies while invigorating pallid, dull skin.

Sea buckthorn is a potent nutritive and regenerative antioxidant. This amazing berry is thought to correct imbalances and improve the health of all skin types. Sea buckthorn may protect against UV damage.

Vitamin E is a natural antioxidant, vitamin E plays a crucial role in protecting the skin from environmental factors.

HEALING SALVES

The solar method is rosemary milk witch's suggest
method. The sun represents LIFE and VITALITY. ma
flowers and herbs wouldn't be here for us to use and l
without the solar energies. So let them rest in oil in
light of the sun. There doesn't seem to be any sort
precise measurement for how much oil and how ma
herbs are needed, but here are the rough instructio:

Place a handful or two of dried herbs in a clean, dry
(make sure it's completely dry – you don't want molc
start growing) and cover the herbs with oil... any car
oil will work. Seal the jar and keep it in a sunny place
a couple of weeks. Give it a shake every so often. Afte
time in the sun, strain the oil with cheesecloth, squee
every bit of oil out of the herbs.

After the oil is ready, it's time to turn it into a baln
Which is totally simple because you're basically ju
combining the oil with beeswax.

HERBS TO USE

Arnica flowers
Burdock root
Calendula flowers
Cayenne powder
Chamomile flowers
Chickweed
Comfrey leaf and/or root
Echinacea herb and/or root
Ginger root
Goldenseal leaf and/or root
Lavender flowers
Myrrh Gum powder
Nettle leaf
Oregon Grape root
Plantain leaf
St. John's Wort
Thyme leaf
Yarrow leaf and flowers

easc note that this is only a partial list, and many other
herbs can also be incorporated into salves. Happy salve
making!

HEALING SALVES

For skin rashes, swelling, wounds, eruptions + burn
calendula . plantain leaf . mugwort . comfrey leaf

For itches and rashes
chickweed . neem oil .
20 drops lavender essential oil
20 drops tea tree essential oil
20 drops rosemary essential oil

To help stop bleeding, and to promote skin
regeneration
yarrow . chamomile . calendula

Try this recipe:
2 cups olive oil or almond oil
1/4 cup beeswax pastilles
1 tsp echinacea root (optional)
2 Tbsp dried comfrey leaf
2 Tbsp dried plantain leaf (herb-not banana!
1 Tbsp dried calendula flowers (optional)
1 tsp dried yarrow flowers (optional)
1 tsp dried rosemary leaf (optional)

HEALING SALVES

SUMMER HIPPY SALVE

This herbal salve is a must have here during the summer when we're dealing with poison ivy and bites or stings. We are aware that you hippies love rolling around completely free in the forests... This recipe yields about 1½ cups of salve, but you can scale it up to make larger batches.

INGREDIENTS

2 cups almond oil or oil blend or any carrier oil
2 tablespoons dried plantain leaf
2 tablespoons dried comfrey leaf or root
2 tablespoons dried burdock root
¼ to ⅓ cup beeswax pellets
1 teaspoon vitamin E oil, optional preservative
20 drops lavender oil, optional

COOKING FOODS WITH HERBS

WITCHY FOOD RECIPES

Gardens and libraries
Gardens and libraries
What book shall I read today?
Gardens and libraries
Gardens and libraries
What faeries will come out to
play?
The tea it will boil
The cookies will bake
The butter and oil
What herbs shall go in the
cake?

HERBS + SPICES
AND THEIR USES

allspice - flavoring cakes, frosting, puddings, soups, sauce, pickles + jellies

anise - seeds for flavoring cookies, pastries, soups, beets, salads, beverages

basil - used fresh or dried for tomatoes, poultry, meats, eggs, soups + sauces

bay leaf - soups, stews, roasts, gravies, sauces, pickles

caraway - flavoring meat and breads

cardamom (rosemary milk witch favvvvv) for flavoring cookies, cakes, candies, all sorts of treats, curries, coffee, teas, kitchari

chamomile - ICE CREAM! YES! ICE CREAM!

lavender - ALSO FOR ICE CREAM! and I'm sure other things. but Ice cream!

cinnamon - literally everything

rosemary - literally everything

ROSEMARY MILK WITCH SHORTBREAD COOKIES

use organic holy ghee to substitute
butter
1 cup of organic cane sugar
3 cups of plant based flour (almond)
tablespoons of the sacred rosemary -
fine chop
dried crumb sage

oven preheat 300
ghee and sugar - check!
add 2 1/2 cups of the flour and mix
a medium bowl, cream together butter and 2/3 cup sugar until
light and fluffy. Stir in flour, salt, and rosemary until well
ended. The dough will be somewhat soft. Roll dough into a log,
wrap with plastic wrap, and refrigerate for at least 1 hour.
Line cookie sheets with parchment paper.
emove dough from the refrigerator. Cut the log into 1/4 inch
hick slices and place cookies 1 inch apart on prepared cookie
sheets. Sprinkle the tops with 2 teaspoons sugar.
ke for 8 minutes or until the cookies are just starting to turn
golden at the edges, Cool on wire racks.

ROSEMARY MILK WITCH PINK SALAD

dressing
1/4 cup cold-pressed flaxseed oil
1/2 cup extra virgin olive oil (or ghee)
1/3 squeezed lemon
just a pinch of mermaid sea salt
large handful of sacred cilantro (fresh
handful of sacred parsley
1 garlic clove (to keep toxic vampires
away while you eat)
2 teaspoons of holy honey (local,
organic, unpasteurized)

salad
2 cups of leafy greens (perfect time to
go harvest those dandelion leaves in
your yard!!)
half a carrot, grated
1 small beet, grated
handful of pumpkin seeds

ROSEMARY MILK WITCH BASIL QUINOA

1 cup quinoa, rinsed to reduce bitterness
1 1/2cups of water
2 tablespoons of coconut oil, divided or
substitute with ghee
LARGE handful of holy basil (fresh)
chop it up
3/4 cups finely diced fresh pineapple or
mango
1/2 teaspoon of sea salt

ROSEMARY MILK WITCH AYURVEDIC KITCHARI

options
vegetables such as zucchini, asparagus
sweet potato, carrot, leafy greens
For Vata or Kapha conditions
add a pinch of ginger powder
For Pitta
leave out the mustard seeds

1/2 cup basmati rice
1 cup mung dal (split yellow)
6 cups (approx.) water
1/2 to 1 inch ginger root, chopped or grated
A bit of mineral salt (1/4 tsp. or so)
2 tsp. ghee
1/2 tsp. coriander powder
1/2 tsp. cumin powder
1/2 tsp. whole cumin seeds
1/2 tsp. mustard seeds
1/2 tsp. turmeric powder
1 pinch asafoetida (hing)
Handful of fresh cilantro leaves
1 and 1/2 cups assorted vegetables (optional)

prep

Carefully pick over rice and dal to remove any stones. Wash each
separately in at least 2 changes of water. Add the 6 cups of water to the
rice and dal and cook covered until it becomes soft, about 20 minutes.
While that is cooking, prepare any vegetables that suit your constitution.
Cut them into smallish pieces. Add the vegetables to the cooked rice and
dal mixture and cook 10 minutes longer.

In a separate saucepan, sauté the seeds in the ghee until they pop. Then
add the other spices. Stir together to release the flavors. Stir the sautéed
spices into the cooked dal, rice, and vegetable mixture. Add the mineral
salt and chopped fresh cilantro and serve.

SYRUPS + TONICS

SYRUP

A syrup is commonly used in treating coughs and sore throats because it will coat the area and keep the herbs in direct contact. add about two ounces of herbs to a quart of water and gently boil down to one point. strain & while warm, add one or two ounces of honey and/or glycerine. licorice and wild cherry bark are two herbs commonly used as therapeutic agents in making syrups. other herbs commonly used in cough syrups are thyme, comfrey root, anise seed, Irish moss, and small amounts of lobelia. syrups are used in doses of one half to one teaspoon as needed.

GRANDMA'S CLASSIC ELDERBERRY SYRUP

cold water 4 cups
dried elderberries 2 cups
cinnamon stick 1
grated ginger root 1 tsp
raw honey

REISHI & ROSE ELDERBERRY

elderberry
reishi
lemon balm
echinacea
rose petal
raw honey
cane alcohol
cinnamon
cardamom
vanilla
nutmeg

IMMUNITY TONIC

reishi
chaga
elderberry
astragalus
rosehips
ginger
cinnamon
raw honey
black cherry

HONEY GINGER TONIC

wildflower honey
apple cider vinegar
ginger root

HONEY MUGWORT

literally just honey +
mugwort

HONEY ROSE

honey
cacao
rose petal
reishi
chaga
vanilla bean
chai

TINCTURES . BITTERS +
DIGESTIVE AIDS

))))) ▶ ◗ ●●●

TINCTURES

highly concentrated herbal extracts thats can be kept for long periods of time because alcohol is a good perspective. the final concentration of alcohol in the tincture should not be less than about 30 % . tinctures are particularly useful for herbs that do not taste good or are to be taken over an extended period of time, and they may be externally used as a liniment. black cohosh and chaparral contain substances not readily extracted by water and thus should be taken in pill form or tincture form rather than teas. tinctures are definitely more powerful than teas. but both are very powerful medicines. combine four ounces of powdered or chopped herbs with one pint of 30 proof or higher vodka, brandy, gin, or rum. shake daily, allowing herbs to extract for up to two weeks. let herbs settle and pour off the tincture. straining through cloth or filter. it is best to put up ones tincture on the new moon and strain on the full moon so that the drawing power of the waxing moon will help extract the herbal properties.

HERBS + SPICES YOU CAN USE

spices
lspice . anise seed . caraway . cardamom . celery seed . cinnamon . cloves . coriander . fennel . ginger . juniper berry . nutmeg . peppercorn . vanilla bean + more

herbs + flowers
amomile . hibiscus . hops . lavender . lemongrass mint . rose . rosemary . sage . thyme . yarrow + more

fruits
lemon . lime. orange . grapefruit . + more

nuts
pecan . walnut . almond . + more

beans
cacao + coffee + more

double extraction is Rosemary Milk Witch's vorite thing ever. chaga, reishi and most of all of our fungi friends that wont harm us.

DANDELION CACAO

cacao 2 tbsp
dandelion 2 tbsp

ORANGE CARDAMOM

orange peel 12 parts
gentian 2 parts
cardamom 2 parts
coriander 2 parts
allspice 1 part
cloves 1 part

ORANGE LAVENDER

lavender 20 parts
orange peel 6 parts
vanilla 2 parts
ginger 1 part

CACAO COFFEE

coffee bean 10 parts
cacao nib 3 parts
wormwood 2 parts
orange peel 1 part
cinnamon 1 part
molasses

GRAPEFRUIT GINGER

grapefruit peel 12 parts
cacao nib 6 parts
ginger 2 part
vanilla bean 1 part
fennel seed 1 part

FIRE CIDERS

DOUBLE, DOUBLE TOIL AND TROUBLE/FIRE BURN AND CAULDRON BUBBLE

As you brace for the dark, cold months ahead. The chill of the earth creates a need for a fire-y herbal potion that wakes up the senses and encourages immune function.

Living in New England, I cannot imagine winter without spicy tea blends, herbal tonics, & warming soups.

One of my favorite remedies that New Englanders swear by is known as Fire Cider. Fire Cider is a traditional remedy with deep roots in folk medicine. This is a recipe that is sure to warm your bones and kick-start your immune and digestive systems.

When I begin my kitchen witchery, I begin by burning sage, palo santo, or cedar to cleanse my space. I like to thank the plants as I use them and try to set an intention of wellness and warmth into my potion. I also love to put on plant medicine music, icaros or kirtan chants.

chop up all your ingredients and place into a clean jar, pour the apple cider vinegar into the jar, topping it off. Then put the lid on. Shake it up! Store in a dark place for one moon cycle.

On the next full moon, strain out the pulp, and pour the vinegar into a clean jar. Be sure to squeeze as much of the liquid goodness as you can from the pulp while straining. Next add the honey. I have Osha honey left over from a wildcrafting trip last summer that I am going to use. Add to taste. I usually incorporate a tablespoon at a time, tasting along the way.

ROSEMARY MILK WITCH FIYAH CIDA

1/2 cup grated ginger root
1/2 cup grated horseradish root
1 medium onion, chopped
10 cloves of garlic crushed
2 jalapeno peppers chopped
1 lemon zest + juice
2 tablespoons dried rosemary leaves
1 tablespoon turmeric
1/4 teaspoon cayenne
apple cider vinegar
1/4 cup raw honey

optional ingredients:
lemongrass . burdock . rosehips . star
anise . thyme . peppercorn . astragalus
. schisandra . parsley . beet root . orange
. grapefruit . lime

ROSEMARY MILK WITCH

→ Find me dancing naked under the full moon with yarrow and rosemary in my hair → Elemental Witch → Virgo-Libra Cusp Sun → Taurus Moon + Rising → 23 years of dancing prayers → casting spells around the sun → Ravenclaw → Butterfly Clan

Priestess of the Goddess

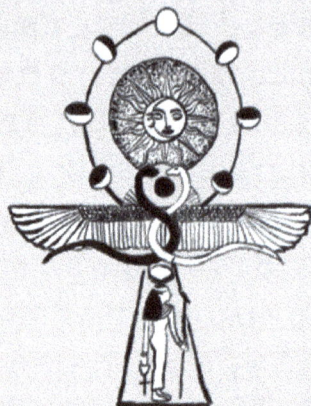

Jedaya Barboza

CREATRESS OF
ROSEMARY MILK WITCH
+
WOMBYN OF THE MOON

@JEDAYABARBOZA
DAYABARBOZA@ICLOUD.COM
PRIESTESSJEDAYA.WEEBLY.COM

cacao ceremony . yoni steaming facilitator . ecstatic dance
. red tent . herbalist witch . intuitive tarot readings

Lightning Source UK Ltd.
Milton Keynes UK
UKHW020059070820
367806UK00001B/11/J